W9-DEG-611

BeCoMiNg MyﬁeLf

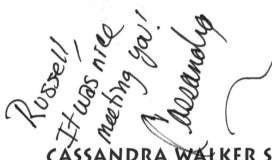

Russel! —
It was nice
meeting you!

Cassandra

CASSANDRA WALKER SIMMONS

EDITED BY PAMELA ESPELAND

Free
Spirit ®
PUBLISHING

Library of Congress Cataloging-in-Publication Data

Simmons, Cassandra Walker, 1966–

    Becoming myself : true stories about learning from life / by Cassandra Walker Simmons.

      p.   cm.

    ISBN 0-915793-69-5

    1. Self-esteem in adolescence—Juvenile literature.

2. Self-esteem in adolescence—Case studies—Juvenile literature. 3. Self-perception in adolescence—Juvenile literature.

4. Simmons, Cassandra Walker, 1966–   . [1. Self-esteem.

2. Self-perception. 3. Adolescence. 4. Simmons, Cassandra Walker, 1966–   .] I. Title.

BF724.3.S36S56   1994

158'.1'0835—dc20   93-44910

                                                CIP

                                                   AC

Cover and book design by MacLean & Tuminelly

10 9 8 7 6 5 4 3 2

Printed in the United States of America

Free Spirit Publishing Inc.
400 First Avenue North, Suite 616
Minneapolis, MN 55401
(612) 338-2068

DEDICATION

TO MY FATHER AND MOTHER, Clinton A. and Odessa Floyd Walker. You gave me continuing love, encouragement, and self-esteem all of my life. I love you both very much.

To my sons, Scott II and Skyler Julius. I love you more than words can say.

ACKNOWLEDGMENTS

THANK YOU, DEAR LORD GOD, for your guidance in putting all of this together. I love you.

Scott, thank you for your time in proofreading and your love during this process.

I want to thank my Aunt Frankye for telling me all those stories when I was growing into a young lady. You inspired me to enjoy reading and storytelling.

Clint II, my only sibling, who would have thought that our memories and crazy days as children would unfold into a self-esteem book? I love you so very much and I am happy that you are my brother and my friend.

I also want to thank my surviving grandmother, Artie Butts, for laughing at all of my jokes and making me feel special. To all the other grandparents on both my and my husband's side of the family—Anne and Julius Floyd, Albert Walker, Laverne and Marcus McGee, Leella and Albin Simmons—thank you for my heritage.

Thank you, Deborah Chiles, for reading my beginning chapters and giving me your honest opinion. Thank you to all of my friends who allowed me to tell about our childhood.

Last but certainly not least, thank you to my in-laws, Larry, Leanna, and Anthony Simmons, for your love and constant support.

Very importantly, thank all of you for investing in my book. May it bless you the way it has blessed me to write it.

A special thanks to everyone at Free Spirit for your help and kindness.

CONTENTS

INTRODUCTION

WHEN I WAS GROWING UP, I WAS OFTEN teased by boys and girls about my lips. Mostly boys did the teasing.

You see, my lips are larger than the average person's, and some people thought they could use this as an excuse to tease me. They would call me "Big Lips," "African Jungle Mouth," "Swollen Lip Face," and so on. I would feel terrible. I felt so bad that I would hold my lips in by biting my bottom lip with my teeth.

I had a horrible complex about my lips. As if that wasn't bad enough, I was also tall and skinny. I prefer the word "thin" myself, but the boys called me "SKINNY."

Of course, the jokes were numerous. "Hey, Cassandra, if you turn sideways and stick out your tongue you will look like a zipper." "You're so skinny you can only fit one stripe on your pajamas." There was also the oldie but goodie, "How's the weather up there?"

The absolute worst was when one boy combined my lips and my weight by saying, "You're so skinny I don't know how you can hold up those big lips."

That time in my life was very painful, but I pulled through. This is how it happened.

One day, my mom noticed me holding in my lips. She said, "You know, in the African-American culture, full lips are normal. They are a part of our heritage—a part of your father and me and our parents and our grandparents...."

Until that minute, I had never heard large lips called "full lips," a much more pleasant term. And I had never even noticed my mother's lips, probably because she didn't try to hide them. They were the same size as mine, and I thought my mom was beautiful.

She told me to be proud of who I was, lips and all. She also told me to look in the encyclopedia and find things and animals that resembled my body size and type. "Gazelles are thin," she said, "and they are beautiful, graceful creatures." And "Look at giraffes! Their tall, thin bodies help them to get food in high places, and everyone loves to look at giraffes."

All of a sudden, it hit me. I could feel the energy inside of me. I no longer looked in the mirror and saw a tall, skinny, big-lipped girl. I saw a tall, thin, graceful, full-lipped African-American beauty.

It took a little while, but soon I learned to love all of me. I would compare myself to other things like long-legged ostriches or tall, beautiful skyscrapers. Whenever I was teased, I would remember these things and feel good about myself.

I also figured out that all of the people who were teasing me had something about themselves that they didn't like. I learned what to do when they teased me. Usually I would answer something like, "You are lucky because you look so great and you're never teased." That would usually catch them off guard and they would stop and think about it. Or I would ignore the teasing and block it out.

I knew I wasn't ugly, inside or out, and I just kept reminding myself. After a few years, we were all older and the teasing stopped. Some of the boys who used to tease me now liked me and wanted to take me out.

Even though the teasing stopped, my self-esteem kept growing and growing, and it still is. Anytime someone says something to me that I find offensive or hurtful, I dig down inside and remember the good things. Now I can look in the mirror and say:

If I believe in myself, I can do it.
If I believe in myself, there's no stopping me.
If I believe in myself, I know I can win.
Believing in myself is where it all begins.

A Message for You

Does the world tell you that you are too thin or too fat? That you have to be like everyone else in order to succeed? That you can't have self-esteem if you don't "fit in"?

This book is designed to help you shatter the world's perception of who you are and what you are supposed to be. You were created to be unique, and unique is what you are. You were born to be a winner and to succeed, and that is what you can do.

Do you believe in yourself? Do you love yourself? Do you have a mind of your own, or do you let others influence your thoughts and actions?

If you answered "no, no, no, yes," you are not alone. I used to be the same way. It is my hope that after you finish reading this book, your answers will be "yes, yes, yes, no."

Enjoy this book. Laugh a little, cry some, and learn from the mistakes I made while growing up. I want you to have enough self-esteem so you can live a fulfilling, happy life and help others do the same.

No one has all the answers, but you may find enough answers here to get you started on the right track to great self-esteem. There is no reason for anyone to have low self-esteem and to not succeed in life.

I had a lot of encouragement at home when I was growing up, and that helped me tremendously. If you don't have that encouragement and you need it, write to me and tell me what your situation is. Let me know what you need encouragement in. I will write back to you, and together we can build your self-esteem.

Write to me at this address:

Free Spirit Publishing
400 First Avenue North, Suite 616
Minneapolis, MN 55401

If you just want to write and let me know how this book has helped you, that's fine, too.

Keep your head up, and remember: *The only thing between you and esteem is self.*

Cassandra Walker Simmons
Spring 1994

1
Changes

THE BIG MOVE

HAVE YOU EVER MOVED TO A NEW NEIGH-borhood? Did you change schools in the middle of a school year? I did when I was 11 years old.

One day my parents came home and said, "Kids, we have good news. We're moving." My brother and I were wondering who this was supposed to be good news for, because it certainly wasn't for us. All I had ever known was the neighborhood where we lived. Didn't my parents realize that I had a vested interest in our block and our school? I guess not, because within two months of their announcement, we moved 35 minutes away from Chicago to a suburb south of the city.

I was terribly upset at having to leave the only friends I had ever known. My parents assured me that I would find new friends and, in the long run, I would like my new life better. Why do parents always use that phrase, "in the long run"? It must be a requirement for all parents to say those words at least once in their lifetime.

On the first weekend after our move, my brother and I sat on the living room floor of our new home and cried for about two hours. Somehow this didn't affect our parents. They just kept setting up the furniture, walking over and around us. No sympathy. My brother and I vowed that we'd show them. We would stick to a code of silence and stubbornness.

On Monday I had to start my new school. I was very worried that I wouldn't fit in with the new crowd. You know how the new kids always stick out.

The first day, my mother drove me, and I got registered and started the sixth grade. My teacher's name was Ms. Bloom and she was very friendly. I told myself, "Teachers are always nice when you are new. Just give it a few days and *pow,* they change from sweet to the Wicked Witch." I knew I had to get a grip and get control. I sat down in my assigned seat and Ms. Bloom introduced me to the class. They all gave me that classroom welcome: "Hello, Cassandra!"

I made it through the day and even managed to laugh a little. I couldn't tell my brother, though, because then I would have broken our code of silence and stubbornness. If he knew I was having a little fun in our new neighborhood, he would surely disapprove.

The next day I was actually looking forward to school. I was still worried that I would somehow mess up, but this time I was ready to conquer the day. I walked down to the bus stop, and as soon as I got there a bus pulled up. A little boy about five years old got on first. I looked around and didn't see anyone else, so I got on, too. As we started on our way, I noticed that all of the kids at stop after stop were kindergarten age or younger. Then I saw some of the kids I recognized from my classroom getting on a different bus. My heart sank and

I started getting really scared. About ten minutes later, we pulled up to a preschool that was attached to a larger building. "This is not my school!" I thought. I was too scared to tell the bus driver, so I got off and walked slowly to the door. Tears just started flying from my eyes. What was I going to do? I didn't even know our new phone number yet, so I couldn't call my parents and tell them I was lost.

Then I saw a sign on the larger building that said "Junior High." I knew that my brother went to the junior high in this area. "Could this be his school?" I wondered. I went inside and found my way to the office. A lady was sitting at the desk. As soon as she asked me what she could do for me, I started crying and shaking. Finally, after about 15 minutes, I was able to say my brother's name, and someone went to find him. When I saw him walk in I was so excited that I ran to him and hugged him. I felt a great sense of relief, knowing that my big brother would take care of me. Then he said, "You are so stupid! How could you take the wrong bus?"

That wasn't exactly what I was expecting. A nice, warm "It will be okay" would have been much more appropriate at this time in my life.

Anyway, someone at the junior high called my school principal and he picked me up. When I got back to school, I thought I would be able to sneak into class unseen. But when I entered, the teacher said, "Oh, the principal told us what happened. We're so glad you made it safely." Everyone in the class started laughing, and I was the most popular topic for jokes for the rest of the week. Actually, it wasn't that bad. It broke the ice between me and many of the other students.

After the first school week, both my brother and I were getting used to our surroundings and starting to understand why our parents had moved us here. Then one day, when we all returned from a family outing, we found that our garage had been spray-painted with the words "Niggers Go Home."

I was shocked and hurt. "Daddy, why would they say that to us?" I asked. My father replied, "They are not talking to us. If you look up the word 'nigger' in the dictionary, it means an ignorant person with little to no knowledge. No one in our family is like that. You always remember that." Then he quietly painted over the graffiti and went inside.

If this incident ever bothered my parents, my brother and I never knew. I was so proud of my parents that day. They could have said very negative things about whoever had painted those words on our garage, but they didn't. They could have gotten us so upset that we withdrew from other people in the neighborhood, but they didn't. Instead, they taught us that we were good people, and we didn't have to let the impressions or words of others affect who we were.

My mother told my teacher about the incident, and we talked about prejudice in class. It was so refreshing to know that my new friends liked me for myself and didn't think of me as strange just because I had a different skin color than most of them.

Sometimes I went back to my old neighborhood and saw my friends there. I still have close relationships with some of them. After the spray-painting incident, I knew that everything was going to be all right. My worry somehow just disappeared.

If you are going through a big change, don't withdraw or choose a code of silence and stubbornness. Open up, meet new people, explore your new surroundings, and don't let worry take over your life.

WHAT'S YOUR PROBLEM?

THERE COMES A TIME IN A YOUNG PERSON'S LIFE when everything seems to go smoothly ...then WHAM, puberty hits.

This strange phenomenon happens to every person on the face of the earth, and you can either adjust to it or hate it. Since it can't be avoided, it seems better to adjust to it—something easier said than done. I know.

My hardest bout with puberty was my hand-eye discoordination. Hand-eye discoordination is what happens mostly to tall people when they grow rapidly. In my case, I grew so fast that my mind couldn't keep up. When I reached for something, my eyes would tell my mind that it was a certain distance away, but my mind would tell my hand that the object was farther away than it actually was. I would knock over juice, boxes, whatever.

My mind was used to my arms being 20 inches long...and now they were 25 inches long. This distance gap made me look and feel awkward. I would go to open the window and bang my hand on it, or reach for the handle on the refrigerator and break my nails. It was so hard for me to do the simplest tasks.

Finally, after hearing me called "clumsy" for so long by the neighborhood kids, my mom took me to the doctor and he explained what was happening. He said that I would "grow out of it" in about a year. A year! I thought, "I don't have a year. Doesn't he know that I'm in love with the cutest boy in my fifth-grade class?" I had to get over this before school started up again.

It would have been easy for me to sit down and cry, and I did for a little while. Soon I realized that if I was going to beat this thing, I had to teach myself. I began by slowly reaching for things so my mind could have time to digest the distance. It was hard at first, because I looked so goofy reaching for a glass of milk in slow motion.

After this started to work, I practiced doing cartwheels. This helped me to judge the distance in reaching down. It may sound stupid, but when your body is out of whack, it is hard to know when to stop trying to reach for the ground. If you misjudge, you end up with bent elbows and a bruised forehead. I practiced all summer long, even through the ridicule of my brother and his immature friends.

By the time school started, I felt prepared. I still remember seeing the then-love-of-my-life standing on the playground. As I approached him, I tried not to think about my condition. I walked right up to him, smiled, stuck out my hand to shake his, and with ever so much gracefulness...poked him right in the eye.

I thought I was going to die.

It wasn't until later that I found out he had still been walking toward me as I was reaching. That was how the accident happened, so it wasn't really my fault. I *had* gotten over my hand-eye discoordination problem. It took a while and a lot of practice, but so does anything else worth doing.

As for the love of my life...well, he didn't think I was the right girl for him, so he ended up with some girl with two left feet.

Whatever your problem may be — growing too fast, reading too slowly, stuttering — if you have the desire to beat it, *you can*.

FROM FROG
TO PRINCE

D O YOUR PARENTS HAVE FRIENDS THEY LIKE to visit? Do they take you with them? Usually when they do it's because their friends have kids, too. And usually the grown-ups assume that you'll be able to play together just because you're kids. But it doesn't always work out that way.

My mother used to take me over to her friends' houses and say, "While I visit, you play with so-and-so." We would stare at each other without the least desire to play together. Call it intuition, but when a boy is pouting and kicking his toys and saying, "I want to play baseball," this probably means that he isn't too overjoyed about a girl coming to visit.

One family we often visited had a girl three or four years younger than me and a boy two years older. The girl was sweet and friendly, but the boy, who was 12, would barely look up at me. He seemed to be very shy and withdrawn, and he always had his head in a book. All I could see were the tops of his black-framed glasses.

One day, during one of our famous visits, we were all watching television. The boy—I'll call him

Jimmy—had his back to me. Whatever we were watching was making us laugh, and we all seemed to relax. Suddenly Jimmy turned around and said, "I love this show. It is so funny." If he said anything else after, that I didn't hear him. All I saw was a face covered in a mound of zits that seemed to lump together in a shape of their own. In front of the zits were some very thick glasses that caused Jimmy's eyes to look like small peas. I was shocked and I must have looked it, because Jimmy stopped talking and turned back around.

I could hardly wait for my mother to finish her visit so I could tell her about what had happened. When we got in the car, I proceeded to ask her if something was wrong with Jimmy. She told me that he had a very bad skin disorder but he was going to see a dermatologist. Then she said that he had been born with a serious eye problem and his parents had just scheduled him for an operation.

"No wonder he always holds his head down," I said. "I mean, who wouldn't?" My mother quickly reminded me that what counts is what is on the *inside*. I knew deep down that this was true, but I also knew that girls had a hard time seeing past a boy's face to get to the inside.

About a year went by, and I hadn't escorted my mother to Jimmy's house even once during that time. I had almost forgotten about him and his situation. Then one day my mother told me that Jimmy and his family had moved very close to us and we were going to visit them. On the way over, she told me that Jimmy was in high school now and doing very well. He was even on the swim team. I thought to myself, "I wonder if chlorine is bad for his skin, and how can he see underwater without his glasses?"

As we approached their house, I tried to mentally prepare myself for greeting Jimmy and his family. I told myself, "I *will not* stare at his face, I *will not* stare at his face." We walked up to the door and knocked and his mother answered. She let us in and we proceeded to the living room area. She told me that Jimmy was upstairs and he would be down shortly. I told her that he didn't have to come down on my account.

The words were barely out of my mouth when he walked into the room. I looked up at him and did just what I said I wouldn't do. I stared at his face. He was gorgeous! His skin had cleared and the glasses were gone. He told me that after he had the operation on his eyes, he was able to wear contact lenses. Not only did his face look great, but he had been lifting weights and he had huge muscles.

Jimmy explained that once he had his operation, he started liking himself and taking better care of himself. Joining the swim team helped him to meet others and to stay in shape. He also said that he had realized that he was a great guy with or without his surgery, and that was the best therapy of all.

Jimmy had turned from a frog to a prince, both inside and out. To tell you the truth, he was never a frog to begin with. I was just too blind to see.

TIN GRIN

WHAT?! I DON'T WANT TO HAVE BRACES!" That is what I told the orthodontist and my mother. They both insisted that I would be so happy...when I had my braces removed. That may be true, I thought, but what about in the meantime? After all, we're talking four years of my life! Think about it. A person gets to be President of the United States for four years. You can graduate from college in four years, and for a 12-year-old, four years is the time it takes to go from riding a bike to driving a car. Four years is a big chunk of anyone's life, and this life was mine.

I must admit that my orthodontist, Dr. Greenfield, was very nice and comforting each time I had to visit him. He also had some excellent stories of people who had braces and how it helped improve their lives. But I couldn't take Dr. Greenfield with me to school. So there I was, all alone, with echoes in my head of "Hey, brace face!" "How's it going, Tin Grin?" and the worst, "Can I put a magnet on your teeth and see if it will stick?"

I'm not going to tell you that I learned to "grin and bear it." I never liked my braces, not for one minute. But when I ran out of tears and had heard all the stupid braces jokes that had ever been thought of, I decided to do something.

I took the attention away from my teeth and put it on me, a person—not a walking braces factory. I styled my hair in new and different ways that drew attention. I took extra care in matching my clothes and wearing accessories like bows and pins. Most of all, instead of being upset and cruel to the people who ridiculed me, I was nice to them and even laughed at some of their braces jokes.

Soon the jokes stopped and I blended in with everyone else. It's no fun for the people who tease you if it doesn't affect you. Also, by taking time to draw attention to other things about myself, I started taking more pride in how I looked, and I have been doing that ever since.

When the braces finally did come off and I looked in the mirror, Dr. Greenfield and my mother were right. I did like my new teeth. Now I can't stop smiling.

CHANGES

WHEN MY BROTHER WAS IN ABOUT THE eighth grade, his voice started to change. It sounded so funny because sometimes it would squeak and crack while he was talking.

He loved playing baseball and had played since he was eight years old. He was considered one of the best pitchers in our area in his age category. Our parents bought him every apparatus invented to help him with his game, and we went to so many Little League games that I thought the hot dog was one of the four basic food groups.

My brother was at the height of his career when his voice started to change, and so did his body. He developed a joint disorder in his knees that they called the "boys' disease." His knee joint started to separate from his marrow and it caused him great discomfort.

It was sad to see him go through such pain and agony. Even more upsetting was the fact that his game was suffering. He couldn't run the bases anymore, so when he hit the ball someone else ran for him. He couldn't do the full workout, so he just watched. By the time he got to high school he couldn't play at all. In one short year, he went from being on top of the Little League world to being on the sidelines, and it ate him up inside. Finally he was cut from the ninth grade team, and his self-esteem fell apart. Nothing made him happy anymore, and he wouldn't communicate with any of our family members. He shut all of his feelings inside himself and left them there.

This caused him to get into mischief. He stopped enjoying school and instead hung out with other kids who didn't have much self-esteem. He went through a long period of getting into trouble and adjusting, and I can't help but think that if only he could have expressed his feelings in some way, he might have avoided the hard times. Instead, he didn't think he had anyone to confide in, and he was tired of being disappointed. He convinced himself that if he didn't work hard at anything and didn't care, he wouldn't have to worry about being disappointed anymore.

Are you going through a difficult time in your life? Is your body out of whack, and does it seem as if you're the only one who is experiencing these changes? You're not the only one, and you're not alone. Please open up your feelings to someone who can help you get through them — a parent, guardian, teacher, or trusted neighbor. You can also go to the library and check out books about the human body. Do whatever it takes until you understand what you are going through. If you have tried all of

these ideas and you are still upset and have nowhere else to turn, write to me and I will help you figure out what you can do. Your life isn't over just because you are changing. Believe it or not, it's only beginning.

2

VaLUes

THE COST OF
BEING COOL

MY PARENTS WERE VERY PROUD OF THE values they instilled in us, such as "don't lie, steal, cheat, or ridicule people." Sure, take all the fun out of being a kid.

I tried my best to live by those values and prided myself in doing so. Some of my friends would tease me and say, "Cassandra, chill out—your parents aren't around." Inside of me, it didn't matter if my parents were around or not. I knew that I had to live with myself, and the only way I could do that and like myself was to stick to my values. Then came high school.

During the first few days of my freshman year, I made some new friends that I had known in junior high but never spent any time with. They were the "cool kids." For some reason, we were all in the same lunch period, which lasted an hour, and we all sat together. Mixed in with the cool kids were a few of us "average kids."

Do you like to be by yourself, or would you rather have a few friends around? With the exception of multiple births, we all come into this world alone, but none of us really likes to be alone. I used to always want people around me. It made me feel accepted.

But it matters who you spend your time with. Even though I knew how to act and how to treat people, I started to change. Whenever I was in the lunchroom with the cool kids, I would get a sort of attitude like they had. All of a sudden I was too good for anyone else. When other kids walked by, we would talk about them or laugh at what they had on. For instance, we would say things like, "The rain is over, the land is dry, so why in the heck are your pants so high?" If someone we didn't particularly like said hello, we would talk about them when they walked away. The whole atmosphere was negative.

It didn't really dawn on me how much I had changed until a friend of mine from junior high sat next to me one day and heard me talking about people. She looked surprised and said, "Boy, Cassandra, you have really changed. I have never heard you say a bad thing about anyone, and now you can't say anything good." I just stared at her. Then, when she left, I talked about her.

One day I was approaching a group of my cool kid friends when I heard them talking about me. I was so mad and upset that I just snuck away before they saw me. I started thinking about how many times other kids might have heard me talk about them and quietly snuck away. It was then that I knew I didn't like who I had become.

I had thought it was fun and good conversation to cut others down and talk about them. Now I realized how very unhappy we were as individuals if we had to get pleasure in putting others down.

Slowly I started finding new friends and new interests. I don't even think the cool kids missed me. They were too busy talking about other kids, probably including me. I went out for cheerleading and started back being the person I used to be, a person with values. I really started liking myself, and that helped me to like others even more.

Recently a friend of mine told me that she had seen one of those former cool kids, and you know what? She was still putting people down, except now she wasn't in a crowd. She was with only one other person. I guess the other kids must have learned, like I did, that some values are not worth giving up if you plan on keeping good friends and being a good person.

Now when I run into people I haven't seen in a while and I tell them what I am up to, they say, "I knew you would do something good with your life, because you have always been a good person." That was and is one of the highest compliments a person can give me. I'm glad they don't remember when I wasn't so good.

I know it seems fun to talk about and tease other people, but the next time you catch yourself doing it, stop and think about what you are doing. Then turn the tables around and think about how you would feel if you were the one

being ridiculed. Also, take a look at the people you hang around with. Do they bring out the best in you or the worst? Do you really enjoy their company, or would you rather be with someone else—or even by yourself? Check these things out, and if they aren't the way you like them, change them. Talk to someone older, someone you trust, and get his or her advice. Or just slowly stop hanging around with those people. You may be alone for a while, but not for long. In the end, you'll have more friends than you can keep track of. I do.

CLEAN UP
THIS MESS!

I HAVEN'T SEEN YOUR ROOM SO I DON'T KNOW WHAT it's like, but I can tell you that mine was a mess. I knew where everything was—I had a system. It was a junky system, but it worked for me.

Every weekend my mother would tell me that I could not go outside until I cleaned up my room. I never knew why it bothered her so much. After all, it was *my* room. Couldn't I at least keep *my* room the way *I* wanted it? "Not in *my* house," my mother would say. "Clean up this mess!"

So I would start my weekly clean-up: Stuff this in a drawer, push that in the closet, and jam these under the bed. There...all done!

After several years of knowing about my stuffing-pushing-and-jamming, my mother decided to try and trick me into cleaning my room. "The cleaner your room, the more new clothes that can fit," she would say. When that didn't work, she dragged all of my things out of every hole and crack I'd hidden them in and put them in a big pile in the center of my room. This was supposed to make it harder for me to get around. I just used the pile as a springboard onto my bed or as a huge, soft pillow to rest my tired body after school. Then one day my mother overheard me tell a friend that the pile in my room didn't bother me a bit. She gave up on this tactic, too.

My friends picked up where she left off. They would come over and say, "We feel bad for your parents. They have a child who doesn't appreciate the lovely home they have provided for her." I would laugh at them. Then they would say, "When you get older, it will be hard for you to keep a clean dorm room in college and a clean house." I pretended that it didn't matter what they said, but deep down, it did. I didn't want people to think I was a slob. Somewhere underneath all that junk, I had pride.

Soon my messy room followed me to school. I had a messy locker and a messy book bag. This made it harder for me to keep my homework organized. My friends started calling me "Messy Marvin." Then one day at school my locker was broken into, and because it was so junky I couldn't tell what had been stolen. I decided I needed a better system. I started trying to keep my room neater. I would try to clean it twice a week instead of waiting until it was a total disaster. At school, I took my time and organized my locker. I felt much better about myself, and my parents felt better also. When I finally did go away to college it was hard for me to keep my dorm room clean, but I was determined to shake the "Messy Marvin" syndrome—and I did.

BECOMING MYSELF

If you have decided that it's time for you to "clean up your act," here are some tips that might help. First, try to clean one section of your room a day—your closet on Monday, under the bed on Tuesday, your desk on Wednesday, and so on. This way it won't get totally out of hand. Next, keep your locker reasonably neat. You'll save time finding the things you need and you might even get better grades. You may have to start by admitting to yourself, like I did, that being messy isn't your "system" or your style. It's just lazy. Then remind yourself that the best part of keeping your room clean is not having to hear your parents scream at you about it.

My friends still tease me when we think about those days, but at least they can't call me "Messy Marvin" anymore.

THE D.D.T. CLUB

I N HIGH SCHOOL, I WAS KNOWN AS A SORT OF goodie two-shoes. It didn't bother me much, and I think that is why I started the D.D.T. Club. D.D.T. stood for "Don't Do That," meaning anything that was mentally or physically unhealthy.

The D.D.T. Club was for girls who didn't want to give into peer pressure to use drugs, smoke, drink alcohol, or have sex. I had seen so many of my classmates in trouble because of drugs and alcohol and too many young girls pregnant. I was determined not to fall into any of those traps.

There were about eight members in the D.D.T. Club at our school. At first some kids made fun of us, especially the boys. Then teachers started recognizing our club and encouraging others to join. Slowly kids started respecting our club and it even grew to other schools, where members wore special T-shirts.

The club gave girls a chance to be proud of who they were and what they stood for. It also let others know where you stood on certain issues. If you started dating someone, he knew you weren't interested in sex and he wouldn't pressure you. If he was the pressuring type, he wouldn't ask you out (thank goodness). Also, when you went to parties no one would hassle you about smoking or drinking. It felt good to belong to the D.D.T. Club.

After we graduated and went on to college, we discontinued the club. Even though we were all adults and could legally drink or make up our minds about other important decisions, the D.D.T. Club had set important precedents for us to follow. We had all made it through adolescence a little easier without the worry of high school pregnancies or drug abuse affecting our lives, and we didn't forget how the club had helped us once we were on our own.

Do you like the idea of a D.D.T. club? Then start one at your school. It may be just what you and your friends need. You might even take it one step further and let boys join, too.

IN STYLE

Don't get the shoes that slip and slide
Get the shoes with the star on the side.

THIS IS THE CHANT WE USED TO SING IN MY neighborhood when I was growing up. I remember my brother and me trying to convince our parents to buy us those name-brand gym shoes. Why should they spend that extra ten dollars? We couldn't come up with even one good reason, so we used the old sympathy stand-by: "Everyone else has them!"

Although everyone else *didn't* have them, our friends did, and that was all that mattered to us. I mean, be for real: How could we show our faces on the playground with anything less than the best on our feet?

I know how important it is to be in "style," especially during adolescence, so I won't say that clothes don't matter. I will say, however, that you can get lost in fashion and lose yourself. Try to stay yourself, even if you are wearing the same things everyone else is wearing.

BECOMING MYSELF

MISERY LOVES COMPANY

Y BROTHER STARTED SMOKING AT about age 12. I remember when an older neighbor who smoked offered him a cigarette. My brother didn't want to say no out of fear that he would not be accepted. So he tried it, and he smoked for 16 years after that. In fact, he just quit about a month ago.

In this type of situation or any situation you feel is wrong for you, listen to your instincts. They will steer you in the right direction. Try not to give in to people who don't have your best interests at heart. They just want to drag you down with them.

As my mother always said, "Misery loves company." This is true for many things, including school work. For example, if you go to a friend's house to study and he decides he wants to play video games instead, he won't feel so bad about getting a poor grade if he has company—you.

My friend, Deborah Chiles, told me a similar story. When she was in junior high, she once let some friends cheat off of her test. She figured that since she wasn't the one cheating, she didn't have anything to worry about. She didn't know that her friends were copying her test word-for-word. When the teacher noticed the identical papers, he gave all of them a zero.

It's not always easy to tell your friends that you don't want to go along with something that feels wrong for you. More than likely, however, other members of the group feel the same way, and they are just waiting for someone to speak up. Be that someone.

THANK YOU, JUDY BLUME

WHEN I TURNED TEN, MY MOTHER bought me the book *Blubber* by Judy Blume. I couldn't wait to read it because I had heard that Judy Blume was an excellent author.

The main character of *Blubber* is a girl who is ridiculed by her classmates for being obese. As I read her story, I felt sympathy for her. I could understand what she was going through because I was often teased for being so thin. I was moved by the story, but I was moved even more by Judy Blume's writing style. She had a way with words that made me feel happy, sad, and excited. I could smell the scents that she described and feel the textures that she mentioned. I wanted to be able to write this way. I wanted to be an author, just like Judy Blume.

Well, I didn't know anything about becoming an author. I figured that you just wrote something and mailed it somewhere and *voila*, it turned into a book. So I whipped out my favorite writing utensil—my aqua blue crayon—and proceeded to write my story. I don't remember what the story was about, but I do remember that it took a long, long time to write it—about an hour. As I was getting it ready for the mailbox, I realized that I had almost forgotten one important detail: Who was I going to mail it to? No problem. I flipped through one of my books until I found what I was looking for, then wrote out the address for Scholastic Books. I could already hear the reporters asking, "So, Cassandra, how does it feel to have a best-selling children's book at the age of ten?"

I asked my mother for a stamp, stuffed my manuscript into an envelope, and placed it ever so gently in the mailbox. Time went by and I didn't hear anything, so eventually I forgot about my book idea. Then one fall day my mother told me that I had some mail. I thought it was a letter from a friend or some junk mail. When I picked it up, I saw the return address: Scholastic Books. I was overjoyed.

When I opened it, there was my manuscript. I couldn't understand why they had sent it back. Then I saw the letter they had sent along with it. The letter started off by thanking me for submitting my work. "This is good," I thought. "They are thanking me and able to recognize talent when they see it." Then I saw the word BUT.

We all know what that word means: Rejection! After the word BUT, I could barely understand what the letter said. I had my mother read it to me, and it boiled down to this: There is a technique to writing a manuscript, and I hadn't followed it. The person who wrote the letter also wasn't too keen on the fact that I had written my story in crayon. Huh...the nerve.

Anyway, I didn't get a book published through Scholastic, but reading *Blubber* was still a turning point in my life. It taught me to treat people the way I wanted to be treated, no matter what. It gave me the idea that I could be an author someday. I think it had a lot to do with the book you're reading now.

3
FAMILY & FRIENDS

GIRLFRIENDS OR JUST FRIENDS?

M Y FATHER USED TO SAY, "YOU'LL MEET many people in a lifetime and gain only a few *true* friends." Think about all of the friends you have made since you started school. How many are you still friends with today? Probably not all of them; maybe only a few. Why is it that during one school year you can't live without a particular friend, and a couple of years later you can barely remember his or her last name? I believe it's because we all change as we get older, and we don't all change in the same ways.

I have a friend I have known since I was two or three years old. As we grew up, we did everything together. We dressed alike most of the time. People often mistook us for twins or cousins. We were inseparable. At one point, we even cut our fingers and said a blood oath. Well, it was only a *half*-blood oath. I was too scared to actually cut my finger, so I just pretended to. After all, it was the principle that mattered, not the blood itself. At least, that's what I was able to convince my friend to believe.

As we grew older, we started to change. Both of us could feel the changes, and they hurt us deeply.

By the time we got to high school, we were very different. We wanted to remain friends, but somehow the gap continued to grow. My friend went to a high school where most kids liked to smoke and drink beer. She started doing these things, too, but I still loved her so much. I decided that since it made me uncomfortable to be with her when she smoked and drank, I had to find other friends, but I would always be there for her if she needed me.

I started looking for people who were more like me. It wasn't hard to find them, because they were doing the same thing. My new friends were my running mates through high school—Lucille, Deborah, Stacie. We ran track, were on the cheerleading squad, and went out together. We remain friends today.

My other friend is still my friend. She may have been upset when we parted, but she soon realized why it had to happen. Just like before, I love her very much, and as we've both matured, we have made some adjustments and continue to be there for each other. We just don't do the same things outside our friendship. But Monique and I still communicate, and as adults we have been able to accept our differences.

There will be times when you have to make some changes in your friendships. Let your head lead you, not your heart. Make sure that you are comfortable with your friends so you don't end up in situations that are bad for you. I know you can do it, and in the end you won't have lost any friendships. You will have gained many more and possibly saved an old one.

STUCK IN
THE MIDDLE

I TRULY BELIEVE THAT BEING A MIDDLE CHILD IS ONE of the most difficult tasks for self-esteem to handle.

I had two sets of cousins, three girls each. Whenever I spent the night with either set, the middle child would always want to be with me the most. When we ate, she would want me to sit next to her. When we went to bed, she would want me to sleep in her bed. The middle child wanted me to like her the most.

One of my middle cousins told me the reason for this behavior. "When you're around, I feel like I have something that is all my own. My older sister gets whatever she wants because she is the oldest, and my younger sister gets a lot of attention because she is the youngest. Me, I just get hand-me-downs and helpful hints."

My middle cousins often felt left out, and sometimes they felt unworthy. They had to try extra hard to be noticed and get a point across. However, they soon learned that if they gave all they had to give and worked to be their best, they were every bit as special as the others.

Are you a "middle"? Do you sometimes feel left out? Try being your best. I promise you will see that you give as much to your family as anyone else, if not more. Don't walk around feeling stuck in the middle. Be the middle child who is happy in the middle.

COMPARISONS

OMETIMES OUR PARENTS GET SO USED TO US KIDS that they forget we are growing up. It's our responsibility to make our feelings known and to speak up for ourselves. In most cases, parents understand.

One thing that parents don't always seem to understand is how much it hurts to be compared to our brothers, sisters, and other relatives—to anyone, in fact. Even simple comparisons can be painful.

Here is an example of what I mean: I have a cousin named Kim who is very smart. She is one year older than I am, and she took the college entrance exam before I did. I wasn't looking forward to the exam as it was, but to follow her score was a sheer horror to me. I have never been good at taking tests that last longer than an hour. My mind just seems to wander.

Sure enough, my cousin received a score of 28 out of 30. Her parents were proud and so were mine. Her high score, plus good grades, allowed her the pick of almost any college in the U.S.

Although I had good grades, I received a score of 12 on my college entrance exam, and I was labeled a dummy. My parents never called me "dumb" or even questioned my score, but I remember one of them saying, "Isn't that the test that Kim got a 28 on?"

Needless to say, I didn't have my pick of colleges, but I did have my pick of self-criticism. Let's see, who will I be today...stupid? lazy? forgetful? dumb? incompetent? In time, I did get through this, and I was accepted into a very nice college. But first I had to make it clear to my family and myself that everyone doesn't do well on tests. Especially not me.

Overall, my parents were extremely good confidence-builders for me, so an occasional slip-up was expected.

SIBLING RIVALRY

WHEN I WAS GROWING UP, I LOVED hearing my brother play the piano. He was very good, and better than very good. He was excellent.

Instead of trying to find out what I was good at, I started playing the piano also. Big mistake. By the time recitals came along, I was still on "Mary Had a Little Lamb" and my brother was playing Beethoven. I wore myself out trying to be just as good or better than he was, but no way.

He had chosen his talent. I had chosen his talent, too, and I couldn't compete. I needed to find my own talent. Soon after I realized this, I took up swimming and cheerleading. I was so much happier doing my own thing.

If you have a talented sibling and you want to be as good as him or her, find your own gift and do your best. Trying to copy your brother or sister can only lead to frustration. Being yourself can only lead to rewards. Remember that you are special and unique. You are different for a reason.

LINGO

EVERY GENERATION HAS ITS OWN LINGO. WHEN my friends and I were in junior high and high school, our whole goal in life was to come up with lingo that our parents wouldn't understand. Sometimes this backfired and we couldn't understand each other.

I remember a time when some of my friends and I were on our way to see a movie. We pulled up next to this very nice white sports car. Whenever we saw something we thought was very nice, we would say it was "smoking" or "smokin'." Well, my girlfriend rolled down the window and told the young driver that his car was "smokin'." He nodded and smiled. His passenger didn't understand our lingo and started screaming, "The car is smoking! Pull over! The car is smoking!"

We couldn't help but laugh. Obviously she didn't know what we meant. She thought the car was on fire. The driver, however, totally understood and he explained it to her.

We even had a lingo especially for clothes. If you wore a coat that wasn't really leather but looked like it, we called it "pleather"—short for "play leather." If you had gym shoes that weren't the latest style, they were "buddies." If you were like me and didn't have designer clothes, your outfits were "generic."

We also had a lingo for dating. If you went out with someone who wasn't your boyfriend or girlfriend, it was called "talking to." If you were dating that person regularly, it was called "going with." It was very important to understand the difference between the two terms. Otherwise you might try to "talk to" someone who was already "going with" someone else. This could lead to a "throw down"—in other words, a fight. Confused? So were we sometimes.

Today I notice that kids use terms like "word" for what we called "straight up" or what our parents called "really" or "truly." So whether it's slammin', whack, dope, down, sweet, or kickin', remember that it's all in good fun. By the way, parents are able to keep up with most of the lingo kids invent. I think they have a guide book.

Whatever your lingo, always be sure to confide in someone if there's something you need to "get off your chest."

4
School

DON'T GIVE UP

IN HIGH SCHOOL, I TOOK AN HONORS ENGLISH class, and I was very excited. I had always liked English, and now I would have the opportunity to do college level work and read advanced novels. I would also get the chance to write creatively. I dreamed of being an author someday, and this would be good practice.

Our first assignment was a book report. I read the book and wrote what I thought was a great report. When the teacher, Ms. Smith, started handing back the papers, I noticed quite a few A's and B's and I could hardly wait to get mine. Then she handed me my paper. A C-minus. WHAT?!

Ms. Smith then told me that she was being generous.

On paper after paper, I couldn't get better than a C. Ms. Smith told me I was being "too creative," so I toned it down. Still a C. Then she said I was being "too wordy," so I cut back. Still a C. After a while I stopped trying and I just turned in any old thing. Still a C.

I had told Ms. Smith that I wanted to be an author. Finally she told me that I should consider another occupation, because I really didn't have what it takes to be a writer and especially not an author. I was crushed.

I almost gave up until I read one of my class-mates' book reports. It was boring and dull. It told exactly what happened in the book, with no inter-pretation or personal reaction. And this was an A paper.

Suddenly it all made sense. Ms. Smith didn't like my reports because I included opinions and suggestions. I tried to make my reports humorous as well as informative. She didn't want to read any-thing but the facts. It was her personal opinion that was giving me C's. Ms. Smith had a style of writing, and mine was not following it.

I decided then that I was going to keep writing like I had been, and one day someone would appre-ciate. I got a C for my final grade, but because it was an honors course it was counted as a B. I knew that Ms. Smith meant me no harm. She just didn't like my writing style. For some reason, she thought her style was the only acceptable one.

I did continue to write. I wrote my way into a reporter's job at a local newspaper. Then I wrote my way into my own children's TV segment on a major television station. I didn't give up, even when someone in authority told me I should.

I have a friend who didn't give up either. Her name is Linda J. Adkins. She went to junior high and high school with me. Here is her story.

Per-se-ver-ance. Such a long word for a young person. "What does it mean?" I asked my father during one of our many "it's-time-to-talk" conversations. He replied, "It means a sense of determination and endurance in the pursuit of a desired goal."

At the time, that wasn't exactly what I was thinking about. I was in high school, where I was a cheerleader, gymnast, student council member, and regular socialite. Why worry about anything besides having fun? Yet I knew there would be life after high school. I was a junior, and it was time to make decisions about my future.

I wanted to become a doctor. This goal seemed sort of comical, coming from someone with mediocre grades. I remember approaching my counselor with the idea. I could see the dismay in his eyes as he searched for a way to tell me that I probably should consider other alternatives. "How about attending the vocational school?" he suggested. "There's a nursing assistance course. Maybe that is what you should consider." Although I was upset that he was not taking my aspirations seriously, I knew I still wanted to become a doctor.

I attended vocational school, and I learned a lot about the medical profession. I reassured myself that I wanted to be a health professional—not a nurses' assistant, lab technician, or therapist, but a doctor. I was positive I could do it. I guess this was perseverance.

I remember a day in high school history class when I almost became discouraged. The teacher informed us that only honor students are expected to become the doctors and lawyers of the future. I knew in my heart that the goals I had set for myself were attainable.

To make a long story short, this is how it goes: After vocational school, I went to college with doubts from everyone including former teachers, counselors, and peers. Even my new college pre-med counselor tried to dissuade me from my career choice. He explained that pre-med was a difficult program and my prior course work was not indicative of a strong science background. I listened politely, yet I was determined to persevere.

It took a tremendous amount of hard work. I sure wished I had paid more attention to class work in junior high and high school instead of focusing on trying to be popular. I had a lot of catching up to do.

I never gave up, and after four years of college and a bachelor of science in biology I was accepted into all the postgraduate schools I applied to. I cried a lot, I often became discouraged, and I didn't graduate at the top of my class, but I did fulfill my dream. I persevered.... Just call me Doctor.

CUTTING CLASS

I REMEMBER GETTING DRESSED FOR SCHOOL AND trying to beat my brother to the bathroom. I took the bus, so I was in a bigger hurry. He had the luxury of driving his car. We would both be ready to go, and I would run and catch my bus. As my bus pulled away, I would see my brother driving down the road...in the opposite direction from our school. Cutting class.

During my brother's most difficult years, he cut class often. I found out about it when someone from the school counseling office called our house one day. I answered the phone and the counselor asked, "Is your brother really sick? Is that why he missed school yesterday?"

I wanted to tell my parents that my brother was cutting class and writing fake notes to cover his tracks. On the other hand, I didn't want to betray him.

There were days when my heart ached for my brother. Until the eighth grade, he was practically a straight-A student. Then he started to change. I missed the old fun-loving him and wished there was some way I could help. I didn't realize that telling on him would have helped.

Soon my parents found out what was going on, and they took my brother's car away. He still kept cutting class, and eventually he wasn't able to graduate from high school.

I never understood why someone would want to cut class. There was nothing to do outside of school except dodge the police. School had so many activities to get involved in, not to mention handsome boys and pretty girls.

Several years later, my brother took the G.E.D.— a high-school equivalency exam—and passed with flying colors. Now he tells others how much time he wasted by cutting class. "It was much harder taking the exam as a crash course than it would have been to go four years with my friends," he says.

School is a lot of hard work, but so is life. If you cut school now, you will be cutting yourself out of a better life in the future. Besides, how are you ever going to buy those fancy clothes you like and those fly athletic shoes if you can't get a decent paying job? I dare you: Go to school and see if you don't amount to something.

ROCK-DIGGER

THE ASSIGNMENT FOR YOU EIGHTH GRADE science students is a book report," said Mrs. Slater.

BOR-ING! I could already imagine 30 students, 30 reports, 30 days of book report torture. Each one would have to be presented orally to the class.

It happened just as I feared...student after student, book after book, bore after bore. To make it worse, my last name was Walker, and we were going in alphabetical order.

Finally I had had enough. I decided that I didn't want my report to be boring. I didn't want to watch my classmates struggle to keep their eyes open as I read from a paper explaining why my book on ROCKS was so TERRIFIC. So when the day finally came to give my report, I borrowed a hardhat and a hammer from my Dad. I filled my school backpack with rocks, put on a flannel shirt and hiking boots, walked into the classroom, and announced, "Hello, everyone! I'm Cassandra, rock-digger *extraordinaire*."

I proceeded to put on a skit and show my classmates actual rock samples that my book described. It was a huge success. My classmates cheered and Mrs. Slater applauded.

That's not all she did. She enjoyed my presentation and enthusiasm so much that she recommended me for an honors high school science class. I was excited, but even more than that, I enjoyed myself. To this day, my former classmates tell me they still remember the names of most of my rocks.

Be creative. Don't always take the easy way out. Think of what you, as a student, would like to see and hear, then try it. The more you allow yourself to be creative, the more creative you will be.

WHO INVENTED ALGEBRA?

HEN I WAS GROWING UP, I WAS OFTEN told that boys were better at math than girls. I remember having to take algebra in the ninth grade. I was never a scholar at regular math, so algebra gave me the heebie-jeebies just thinking about it.

To make matters even worse, our teacher was a man who had taught Earth Sciences the year before. Some science teachers are full of energy and are very interesting. This one wasn't.

I really tried to understand what he was talking about, but I became lost somewhere between "x + 8 = y" and "what is the value of x?" Correct me if I'm wrong, but when did letters start equaling numbers? Somehow I felt I was in the Twilight Zone and couldn't get out.

Even more humiliating was the fact that every time the teacher gave out a problem, he would only let us have three minutes to figure it out. All the other kids would start writing and erasing and all I could do was look like I was in a daze. In fact, I was in a daze.

One time we had a test and when we got the results, I had received a zero. A big, fat, red zero.

I didn't even get an "x = whatever right." I was so embarrassed and upset. A boy next to me shouted out, "DANG, you got a zero! We have been in class six weeks and you didn't get anything right?" Why do people ask questions when they know the answers? It was obvious I didn't get anything right. That is what a zero means.

At this point, I decided to swallow what was left of my pride and get a tutor. This sounds like a good move, doesn't it? Well, my tutor was my algebra teacher. UGH! After six more grueling weeks, I was able to understand what he had been explaining in class. Finally it was coming to me, and by the end of the term I received a passing grade in algebra.

I didn't give up, even when I was at my lowest point. I knew that boys were not necessarily smarter than girls in math. I also knew that if others could understand algebra, I could, too. I'm still not a math whiz, but I'm really good at value grocery shopping and figuring out discount percentages on clothes.

No matter what your circumstances are in school or in life, determination not to be defeated—not to take the zero—will drive you toward success.

LOST IN THE MAZE

MY FIRST DAY OF HIGH SCHOOL WAS almost a disaster. I remember walking into the building. Everything was so huge. It looked like a forest of lockers and students.

My brother was supposed to be my tour guide. My parents had told him during breakfast that he was to walk me to my locker and all of my classes. He had nodded his head.

I was concerned about leaving junior high. I had started to find myself there, and I felt confident walking to classes and talking to teachers. I was on the pom-pon squad and I knew just about every kid in the school. Yep, junior high was my home. Then it ended.

I felt like I was lost in a huge maze. There would be no more speaking to everyone in the hallway as we passed each other going to classes. I didn't know that many kids at my new school. How was I going to manage? Besides all of that, my junior high had about 500 kids in it. This school had three times that many.

At least I would have my brother to escort me around. After all, he was a junior and he knew everyone. I was in good hands. As we passed through the front door, I turned to tell him how thankful I was that he was there to help me. "See ya, Slim," he said. "I'm going to find my friends. I can't be caught in the halls with a freshman. Especially one that is my sister."

"But what about finding my locker?" I screamed. To that he yelled as he was running down the hall, "Look for the number on your locker slip. Oh, and have a nice day."

Just what I needed. As I was being bumped around in the overly crowded hallways, I tried to find locker 1320. Finally, after about twenty minutes, I found it, but my combination wouldn't unlock the lock. "This must be broken," I said. Then a voice answered, "It's not, but you will be if you don't get away from my locker." I looked up to see a very tall, very mean-looking girl staring down at me. I could tell by her expression that she wasn't part of the freshman welcoming committee.

"This is *my* locker," I managed to squeak out. "No, it isn't," she said. "Let me see your locker slip." She took my paper, glanced at the numbers, and started to laugh. "Your locker is in the orange hall. That's what this small 'O' means. You are now in the yellow hall."

I graciously took my paper and started for the orange hall. "They really should go over all of this in orientation," I thought to myself. Finally I found my locker, and after that all of my classes, and I actually made it through the day. After a few weeks I started to meet new friends who were as scared as I was. We hit it off great.

By the time I graduated four years later, I was involved in cheerleading and track, the student council, nurses' aides, and a long list of other activities. It was just a matter of adjusting and growing up—something we have to do all of our lives.

What about my brother? He came to see me at the end of the day. "How did it go?" he asked. I rolled my eyes and said, "Just fine." He gave a smile and said, "I knew you could do it if I left you alone." In the back of my mind, I knew he was saying that so I wouldn't go home and tell our parents what he had done. Still, I did get through the day, and I have been managing to figure out things on my own for the most part ever since.

Will you be starting high school soon? Are you a little scared? Try visiting the school before the first day of classes. During orientation, take a lot of notes and ask a lot of questions. Read the student handbook. I know you'll do just fine.

5
Coping

GROWTH SPURT

THIRD GRADE. EIGHT AND A HALF YEARS OLD. Wow, I'm really living now. I rushed my brother through breakfast so we could get to school. We went to a private Lutheran school with about 150 children from grades K through 8.

When we arrived at our classrooms, I was devastated to learn that I was the only girl in the third grade. And I was taller than the boys.

This is when the pressure really hit. I had to be just as competitive as the boys in school work and in sports, so I had to work twice as hard.

I made the best out of a bad situation. After a while, I gained the respect of the boys in class and on the playground.

When you feel outnumbered in a good but awkward situation, befriend the so-called enemy. Learn how to do things their way, and soon they will look at you as different but equal. Keep your head up and do your research — whether you're learning to play baseball better or recite math problems faster. That way you can always stay one step ahead.

GETTING A GRIP ON DEPRESSION

DEPRESSION COMES IN ALL SHAPES AND SIZES and for all kinds of reasons. In my case, it seemed like whenever I got over one depressing incident, another came along. I had to learn how to deal with depression and get a grip in it so it wouldn't grip me. Everyone goes through some sort of depression in their lives, but not everyone can get over it. I hope my experience can help you find ways to get over your depression and on with your life.

One major cause of depression for me was wanting to be liked by boys. In junior high, it seemed as though all of the boys liked the more shapely girls who wore makeup. Well, I was as thin as a rail, and the closest I came to makeup was strawberry lip gloss.

So there I was, a skinny, shiny-lipped seventh grader with no boyfriend. I didn't really want a boyfriend to date. I just wanted someone to be interested in me. I would get depressed just thinking about it.

I remember having a crush on a boy named Kenny Rogers (no, not the singer). I thought he was so good-looking. When I finally worked up the nerve to tell him I liked him, he looked at me, laughed, and said, "Who, you? Like me?" It felt like a scene from a Tarzan movie—"Me Tarzan, you Jane." Kenny went on to tell me that I was "too tall for him" and "it just wouldn't work." What a blow to my ego! I cried for days. I was convinced that I was ugly and no one would ever like me. Seeing the other more curvaceous girls with all the boys drooling over them didn't help my self-esteem any. I kept wondering, "What do they have that I don't?" I guess it was obvious.

I let this upset me so much that I could hardly concentrate in school. I wondered if anyone else felt like me. Then, as if things weren't bad enough, I lost my appetite and began losing weight. Now I looked like Olive Oyl from the "Popeye" cartoons.

One day in class, I looked over at Kenny and thought, "He isn't worth getting depressed over. There are so many other boys out there." I started realizing how my depression was affecting my school and home life. Then I confided in a friend and told her what I had been going through. "You like Kenny Rogers?" she asked me. "Stop worrying about him. A lot of people like you. Why are you letting Kenny get you down?"

After that I could think clearly again. "Yeah," I told myself, "I am special, and a lot of people like me. Most of them may be teachers and female friends, but hey, it's a start." I still liked Kenny some, but whenever the depression would start to come back, I would focus my mind on the positive things in my life. Like the A on my spelling test, my new coat, and that day in the future when

I would finally fill out and Kenny would want to date me and I would say TOO LATE! (Just kidding!)

I also stopped taking things so personally. Maybe Kenny didn't like me, but that didn't mean I was unattractive. It just meant he didn't particularly care for me. Who was he, anyway, the author of *Who's Who in Seventh Grade Dating?* No, he was not.

Finally I started liking the "just okay" things about me and my life, along with the good things. Yes, I was a tad bit thin, but so are many famous models. Yes, I was tall and I wasn't allowed to wear makeup, but I could swing a mean bat in softball. Hey, I wasn't that bad after all...as a matter of fact, I was kind of fantastic. Kenny was just too short to get a good look at me.

If you get depressed, find someone to talk to. Someone you trust. That person can help you remember the good things about your life. Then write down all of your good points. (Be sure to get a lot of paper. You'll need it.) If you like, you can even write down your goals. Whatever is depressing you in the present will start to look small when you see how bright your future is. Lastly, try not to take things too personally. Just because a certain person or group doesn't accept you doesn't mean that there is something wrong with you. It's their problem, not yours. They are missing out on something terrific if they aren't including you in their lives.

Most of all, remember that you are special. Everything about you is special. So don't stay stuck in depression. Get a grip on it, then get out and enjoy life. It's waiting for you.

FOUR EYES

HEN I WAS GROWING UP, IF YOU WORE glasses you were the playground joke most of the time. "Four eyes, four eyes" is what the other kids called you. To be honest, I wanted to wear glasses because I thought they made you look smart.

A close friend of mine named Terri Townes didn't agree with me. She hated glasses, so when she found out she had to wear them she was very upset. Terri had a weak eye that sometimes crossed. Even though the other kids teased her about having a crossed eye, she felt that was better than wearing glasses.

Terri told me, "I'm mad that I have to wear glasses. No one else in our class wears them." She decided to take matters into her own hands. When she first got her glasses, she conveniently lost them—once in my house, and another time in a deep, deep hole in her back yard. Then there was the time when she lost them where many people lose their glasses: in the corner mailbox. Terri was determined not to wear those glasses.

One day we held bike races in the middle of our street. An older boy stood at the end of the street with his arms outstretched. The first rider to race up to him and touch his hand won the race. Two riders went at the same time.

Finally it was my turn. My opponent was Terri. We sat tall on our bikes and took off when we heard the word "GO." I remember going so fast I could hear the air rushing past me and smell the rubber on the tires hitting the road. Terri and I were neck-and-neck and almost at the end when I saw her sway very close to me. I slowed down. Then she headed straight for the boy who marked the finish line. There was no time for him to run, so he just tried to jump out of the way. Terri's front wheel hit him on his side, forcing him to the ground.

He got up and started screaming, "Why did you hit me?" Terri just apologized and motioned for me to follow her.

As we walked our bikes back down the block, Terri told me that she thought she might start wearing her glasses from now on. I asked her why the sudden change of attitude. "Sandy," she said, as she often called me, "I could have really hurt that boy today. The reason I ran into him was because I started to lose focus in my vision. I saw two of him and I tried to ride through the middle." I thought I would die laughing.

Although this seemed humorous to me at the time, it really was a serious matter. Not only did Terri need glasses for her own health, but also for the safety of others.

I still don't need glasses, but some of my friends do. Like Horace Grant of the Chicago Bulls. When I first met him, he used to squint at the television. Finally he decided he should get glasses, and his basketball game has never been better. He even gets comments on how hip his athletic glasses are.

Look around you and you'll probably see that a lot of people you admire and respect wear glasses. If you ask, you'll probably learn that at one time in their lives they were called "four eyes." If you have to wear glasses but detest them, try to do something inventive with them. Get cool frames that accentuate your personality, or have your parents buy you a nice case to hold your glasses when you are not wearing them.

FOLLOW THE LEADER

HAVE YOU EVER BELONGED TO A SOCIAL group or team that made a lot of demands on you or caused great pressure in your life? What if you are the captain of the basketball or football team? Your teammates are looking to you for guidance. They may even blame you if they lose a game. Pressure!

One way to cope is to delegate some of your authority. Have various members of your group or team serve as subcaptains. Then there will be more than one person to call the shots.

When I was a junior in high school, I was the captain of our cheerleading squad. At first I was extremely happy about being captain, but soon the conflicts began to emerge. Since the other cheerleaders were my peers and close friends, they had a hard time following my instructions, sometimes because of jealousy and sometimes because they didn't take me seriously.

Once I wanted to start practicing and no one would be quiet and cooperate. After half an hour of pleading and yelling, I finally said, "Whoever doesn't shut up NOW and start practicing will be sidelined for the next game!" The others weren't happy with my sudden outburst, but they knew I was serious.

I had to separate myself from my friends and be their leader. This was very hard for me to do. One of the biggest pressures of all is having to lead a group of your peers after you have been at the same level. Unfortunately, this is required in all captain positions. Fortunately, once your friends figure out that you're just doing your job and you're not trying to boss them, just lead them, they will usually start cooperating.

Have confidence in yourself and your abilities to lead. After all, that is why you were chosen. And learn to say no. It's a simple word, only two letters long, but it's very hard to say when someone is asking you for help.

Imagine that you're already busy, with no time to spare. Someone asks you to volunteer some time for an important cause. Can you say no? Most people have a hard time with this, even when saying yes disrupts their lives.

If you say yes too often, try these three strategies:

1. Take a deep breath and ask yourself, "Can I really do this? Do I really want to do this?"
2. If you don't want to help, or you can't help, admit it.
3. Politely say, "I'm sorry, but I can't at this time." Or "I'm not really interested in doing that right now."

Most times, the person doing the asking will understand and appreciate your honesty.

HOME ALONE

USED TO LOVE TO GO TO SCARY MOVIES. I SAW *Friday the 13th* parts 1 through 8 and *Nightmare on Elm Street* 1, 2, 3, and 4. I liked being scared and feeling my adrenaline flow at light speed. But when I got home, all those scary thoughts and images came back to haunt me.

When I was 14 years old, a freshman in high school, my parents started their own business. They had to go to several meetings during the week nights. My brother was supposed to keep an eye me, but he had turned 16 and had a car and a life that didn't include me.

We had a German shepherd named Joe who was supposed to be my watch dog. I say "supposed to be" because, although he was very protective, he was blind in one eye. Nonetheless, he was a good companion. When my parents would leave for one of their meetings, Joe and I would go upstairs to their room and settle in for the night.

Why is it that you only notice the creaks and cracking of the house when you are there alone? It never failed. I would hear all sorts of noises, and then I would start thinking about Jason from *Friday the 13th*. You know, they never *really* killed him. To me, this meant there was a possibility that he was lurking outside of my home, waiting for the perfect opportunity to strike.... This is how my mind would work all night.

I didn't tell my friends about my fears. I was sure they would think I was a big baby who was afraid of staying home alone at night. In fact, that's what I was.

One day my brother snuck up on me and scared me so bad that I became physically ill. I decided that I couldn't continue to be such a worry-wart and a chicken. So I did what any 14-year-old would do: I started a phone chain. I picked up my phone book and called everyone I knew (locally) and talked to them until they had to go. Somehow just having someone to talk to made me feel safe. It also didn't hurt to know that if something did happen they would know about it and they could call the police. It's always good to have a plan B.

Soon I was older and my parents were going out less and I became comfortable at staying home alone. Now that I am a parent, when my husband is out late and it's just me and the kids home alone, I have to be strong. I don't call people on the phone anymore, but I do read a book or I go to bed early and just rest assured that we are safe.

I also keep a large stick nearby. Plan B.

Are you ever afraid of being home alone? Do you have a plan B? Don't waste time worrying about what scary things could happen. Instead, come up with some fun things to do to keep your mind occupied. After all, how often do you have the house all to yourself?

ROBBED!

I T HAD BEEN A YEAR SINCE WE MOVED INTO OUR NEW home, and everyone was settled in. I was in junior high now and my brother was a freshman in high school. One day I stayed home from school because I was fighting a bout with tonsillitis, which I had every year of my life since age three. (By the way, I *finally* got my tonsils taken out—at age 27!)

I locked the dog in the basement so he wouldn't climb all over me. I had fallen asleep on the family room couch when I woke up to a knocking at the door. By the time I got up and made it to the door, I saw two teenage boys walking away. I figured they were trying to sell something, so I just went back to the couch and fell asleep again. Two days later I was better, so I returned to school. I remember being the last one to leave that morning. I had put the dog in the basement while I was getting ready for school, and in my haste I forgot to let him out.

When I got home that afternoon, I opened the door and my mom was there to greet me. "Don't touch anything," she ordered. "We've been robbed."

I couldn't believe it. One of the reasons we had moved was to be in a safer environment.

Chills ran down my spine as I listened to my mother tell the police what she had found when she came home from work. "I had some groceries in the car so it took me longer than usual to get into the house," she said. "When I walked in from the door to the garage, I noticed a large butcher knife on the floor. Then I heard the front door slam and I saw two boys run past the garage. I knew then that we had been robbed and that the butcher knife was intended for me. I guess I took too long so they decided to make a run for it."

The police went all through the house, dusting for fingerprints. Everything in the house was a mess. The robbers had dumped out drawers and closets looking for money and jewelry. The police found out later that the robbers were teenagers who used our house as a hangout all day. Luckily our dog was okay, but because he was in the basement he couldn't get out and attack them.

I couldn't sleep well for weeks. Every time it got dark, I would think that someone was coming for us. I slept in my brother's bedroom on his top bunk for two weeks.

I felt very violated, as if our close, safe family setting didn't exist anymore. I wondered if the robbers had gone through my diary or used my toothbrush. I felt that my home was no longer mine anymore. It belonged to strangers.

Eventually time helped me to get over my fears. My parents bought a burglar system and that helped also. The police figured that the robbers had been casing our neighborhood, and they were the ones who had come by our house the day I was home sick.

I could have let this experience make me a very insecure person. After a while, however, I started to understand that the robbers were the ones who were insecure, and in a strange way, they were the real victims.

I hope you are never robbed, but if you are, I know you will find the strength to get through it. If you are ever tempted to steal from someone, stop and think about how you would feel if it happened to you or your family. Stop and think about how you would feel about yourself after doing such a thing. In the end, it's more than just the people who are robbed who suffer.

WORRY

USED TO HAVE NIGHTMARES ABOUT MY PARENTS dying suddenly. I don't know why I had these nightmares, but I do know they terrified me.

When I was about 12 years old, I met a boy who had lost both of his parents in a car accident. He was an infant when it happened, so he didn't remember any of it. His uncle and aunt took him in and raised him. They had two daughters of their own, and the boy fit in very nicely. My mother and father knew his parents before they died. I often wondered how he dealt with not having parents.

As I grew older, my worry about my own parents increased. If I came home from school and there was no one there, I would panic. If my parents weren't home within 15 or 20 minutes, I would start to cry. In the back of my mind was the thought that they had been in an accident and no one knew how to contact me and my brother. Of course, my parents would eventually return home, and I would feel better. My mother tried to tell me not to worry, but that didn't help. It was terrible to live like this, but I couldn't stop the cycle of worry.

One day my mother said to me, "When I was a little girl, my mother told me that none of us can add another day to our lives by worrying. Worrying doesn't solve any situation or problem. It only creates more problems. You have to come up with your own solution. Worry can cause you to go out of your mind with fear"—which is what I almost did.

I tried to apply what my grandmother said, and it worked. Instead of worrying about my parents, I would clean up the house or do homework—anything to keep my mind off the fact that they weren't home. Before I knew it, they had arrived safely.

Sometimes our worst fears become reality. We worry about someone and that person dies or is injured. But worrying didn't cause the problem and it doesn't solve anything. You still have to deal with the situation. You still need to focus your mind on healthy thoughts. As someone once said, 95 percent of the things we worry about never come to pass, and the other 5 percent we have no control over anyway.

Here are some tips that may help you to avoid worrying:

1. Write down what is worrying you. Put the piece of paper under your pillow or in a drawer for five days. By then the issue will probably be resolved or you will have found a rational solution.

2. Ask yourself, "How is worrying about the situation helping?" When you realize that it isn't helping, figure out something you can do that *will* help.

3. If you can talk to your parents, do so. Ask them for help. If you can't talk to your parents, find another adult you can trust and talk to him or her. The two of you will probably come up with a wise plan for dealing with your worry.
4. Remember: Worry is an emotion, not a problem-solver.

6

DaNGer ZONES

MESSAGE IN
THE BOTTLE

HAVE YOU SEEN ANY OF THOSE HEALTH movies that teach students about the effects of alcohol and why we shouldn't drink? I remember watching one of those films in the sixth grade. This particular movie showed a 12-year-old girl who had a drinking problem. She would ride around the neighborhood on her bike with a bottle of wine in her front basket. The bottle was hidden under a sweater, but the other kids and parents starting suspecting that she was drinking. Eventually the girl crashed her bike when she was drunk. Afterward, she got help, and she was able to function again in school and in society.

The movie was supposed to scare us into not drinking, but it did just the opposite for me. I thought it looked like fun when the girl was drinking out of the bottle. I went home and decided to try it myself.

My parents weren't home yet, so I went into their small wine cabinet and found a dusty bottle. I opened it and put my mouth around the top and turned the bottle upside down. The minute the wine hit my mouth, I started gagging. It was TERRIBLE. My head was spinning as I ran to the sink and spit the wine out. I felt sick. I couldn't understand why my parents even liked to drink that stuff. It tasted like poison to me.

By the time my mother came home, I had put the wine back, but the smell was still there. She asked me who had been drinking and I said, "I don't know." As soon as I opened my mouth, my mother could smell the wine on my breath. She was shocked. She took me into her room and told me about the effects that abusing alcohol could have on a person. She told me how children who drink can and do stunt their growth and slow down their learning rate. She should know, because she is a registered nursing manager for the alcoholic ward at a major hospital in Chicago.

My mother went on to tell me how many young lives she had seen wasted away because of alcohol. She explained that unfortunately some people use alcohol as a way to have fun in life. Then she said that alcohol is a depressant—that it slows down your bodily functions and actually makes you sad, not happy.

It was then that I decided to get high on life, not alcohol.

I know that a lot of young people drink, and I can't tell you what to do, but I would like to make a suggestion. The next time you're around young people who are drinking or drunk, observe them carefully. Do they really look like they are having fun? Do they really look cool, or is it all a put-on? I am sure you will be able to decide for yourself if alcohol is everything the ads and commercials make it up to be.

COUGHING FIT

I HAVE NEVER TRIED SMOKING ANYTHING, NOT EVEN A cigarette. I think it's because my father smoked until I was ten years old, and I hated his smoking. Once I even took his cartons of cigarettes and stuffed them in a bathtub full of water. You have never seen a man so mad. He could have blown fire out of his nose. Then one day he decided that he wanted to quit smoking after 25 years, and he did just that. He hasn't smoked a cigarette since 1976. Now he can't stand the smell of smoke.

One summer vacation, while visiting my grandmother, I met a new cousin. She wanted to show me around the neighborhood, so we went by her house. Before long, her boyfriend came by, and she asked me to go for a ride with them in his car. I was only 13, my cousin was 14, and her boyfriend was about 16 or 17. I felt a little intimidated by him, but I thought my cousin would take care of me.

After about an hour of driving, I asked my cousin where we were going. "To buy some dope," she said. I wasn't sure if she was serious, so I asked her again, and she repeated the same answer. Suddenly I became very scared. My hands started to sweat as we pulled up to a run-down house with about ten people standing outside the front door.

My cousin got out and started talking to the people like she had known them for a long time. Then she and her boyfriend got back in the car with some marijuana and tried to get me to take a puff.

I suddenly remembered an acting class from school. The teacher had often told us, "Always convince your audience that you are whatever character you play." I decided to get "in character." I started to cough and gasp for air.

"What's wrong?" my cousin asked me.

"I'm (cough) allergic to smoke (cough), and I'm getting sick (cough)," I answered. She and her boyfriend looked at me like I was joking. Then I started shaking all over. They became concerned and threw the marijuana out of the car. I told them I had to get back to Grandma's house right away or I might die. In between gasps and shaking, I said, "This has happened only once before, and I had to go to the hospital."

I have never seen two people look more afraid. My cousin's boyfriend drove so fast that I thought the doors would fly off the car. When we arrived at my grandmother's, they begged me not to say anything about what had happened, and I didn't. I finally told my grandmother some years later.

You see, it isn't only strangers who hang out on street corners who try to get us to do drugs. In some cases, it is our relatives or friends—people we trust. I don't believe that my cousin wanted to hurt me. She was just lost, and she had conditioned herself to think that using drugs was okay. She wanted me to share what she thought was "fun."

You might run into a situation like this. If someone tries to force you to smoke or drink, fake getting sick. Really sick. Deathly sick. No one wants to have a dead body on their hands.

You may have heard the old saying, "Misery loves company." It's the same with drugs and alcohol. People who use them want someone else to get hooked so they won't be alone. Don't let them get you hooked. Instead, try to get them unhooked, because inside they are crying for help.

My cousin ended up dropping her boyfriend. I found out later that he had talked her into doing drugs. She never really wanted to, but she didn't know how to say no or fake it.

WHY ARE YOU TOUCHING ME?

DO YOU HAVE FRIENDS YOU HAVE KNOWN FOR a long time but don't see anymore? Maybe you go to different schools or live in different neighborhoods. Whatever the reason, you lose touch...and then one day you get together again.

I always feel awkward when I have to entertain a friend I haven't seen in a while. It can be hard to keep a conversation going. Also, people change, and not always in ways you can understand or cope with.

One day when I was 12, my mother told me that I was going to have a surprise visitor, a friend I hadn't seen for years She went on to say that Sally (not her real name) and her mother would be coming by our house that afternoon. I was excited about seeing Sally again. It had been so long since we had been together.

Sally was a year older than me and kind of quiet. She was an only child, and she didn't seem to have many friends. I don't know how our parents knew each other, but I enjoyed spending time with her. She always came up with creative things for us to do, like making *papier-mâché* or mudpies.

When Sally and her mother arrived, I took Sally up to show her my room. They had never been to our new home. We sat on the floor and talked about what had been happening in our lives. I was surprised at how mature Sally looked. She was much taller now and had started to fill out like a woman. She even wore makeup. I suggested that we play a board game and asked her which one she wanted to play.

As I started to get up, she grabbed my arm and said, "Wait. I have a better game. A new game." I smiled because I knew how creative she was. Then she said, "Why don't you sit down next to me? You know I have always liked you. You understand me.

"I have a new girlfriend who reminds me of you," Sally went on. "My new friend really likes me, and she shows me how much she likes me. Do you like me?"

"Of course I do," I said.

"Do you want to show me?" she asked.

I started feeling strange inside and I didn't know why. Then Sally grabbed my hand and placed it on her breast. "It makes me feel good when my other friend rubs my breast," she said.

"Why would your friend want to rub your breast?" I wanted to know.

"It's a private way to show affection," she said. "I would show you, but you don't have any breasts yet."

By now I was feeling sick inside and afraid. I took my hand away and Sally started taking off her shirt.

"Wait," I said. "I don't want to do that."

"You're acting immature," she said.

"I *am* immature," I said. "I'm 12 years old."

"All girls your age do this," she insisted. "There's nothing wrong with it." Then she tried to climb on me.

I pushed her off and ran downstairs. I was too afraid to say anything to my mother, so I just sat there by her until Sally came downstairs.

Our mothers asked us what was wrong and Sally quickly said, "Oh, Cassandra is being silly." I just looked at her. After that, anytime my mom went to visit them, I refused to go.

It was many years before I told my mother what really happened that day. For a long time, I didn't understand what had gone on between Sally and me. Then one day in health class the teacher talked about "inappropriate touching." I thought back to Sally and realized that was what she was doing and trying to get me to do.

I don't know if anything like this has ever happened to you, but if it does, don't wait even one minute—run to safety. The person might be a friend or a relative. He or she might try to make you feel guilty, ashamed, or confused, but don't listen. Your inner feelings will tell you that the touching is wrong, just like mine told me.

When I was older, I was able to understand that someone in Sally's life had probably done the same thing to her, and that is why she did it to me. I wish I had told my mother or her mother right away. Then one or both of them could have helped her.

Recently my mother told me that she spoke with Sally's mother, and Sally isn't leading a healthy adult life. She is on drugs. I know it is not my fault that Sally is on drugs, but I wish I had spoken up a long time ago.

If you are ever approached by someone who tries inappropriate touching, tell an adult immediately. Don't wait. You'll be helping yourself, and you may be helping the other person, who is probably lonely and scared inside. You might even change the person's life.

A WAY OF LIFE

B Y THE TIME I BECAME A TEENAGER, I HAD met several new and interesting people. I also still managed to keep most of my same friends from junior high. One day, one of my new friends told me that she used to smoke marijuana. She knew that I didn't smoke anything, and she told me she had stopped because she knew it wasn't any good for her.

We spent a lot of time together and I never saw her smoke. We even talked about how bad we felt for some of our other friends who smoked.

One night, my friend and I went to an all-girls sleepover party. A lot of different girls were there. Some I knew very well, and others I hardly knew. I remember going downstairs to play a word game with some of the girls. After a while, I realized that I hadn't seen my friend in a long time. I started walking through the house and I heard some talking in a room. When I opened the door, the room was filled with smoke, and I saw my friend. She looked at me and giggled. She had obviously been smoking marijuana.

I left the room and went back downstairs. A few minutes later, she came down and asked me, "Why didn't you come in the room?" She asked as if she thought I couldn't tell she had been smoking. I answered, "You know why."

She stared at me with red eyes, and then she looked down at the floor. I could feel the guilt coming from her.

The next day she pulled me aside and apologized for smoking. "There is no apology necessary," I told her. "You are old enough to make your own decisions." She explained that she had given into peer pressure and her old way of thinking. Everyone in her neighborhood smoked marijuana, she said, and it was just a way of life. Then she met me and realized there was more to life.

I had never thought about the social pressures of the way you were brought up and how it could affect your actions and decisions. I apologized to my friend for just assuming that she had a strong family to support her in not using drugs or alcohol. We hugged, and as far as I know she has never used drugs again.

When you meet people in your lifetime, you will find that not everyone has had the opportunity to be in a drug-free, abuse-free environment. Some people's families use drugs or alcohol heavily. Your family might be like this. If so, remember that you don't have to be the same way. You can find other people who, like you, don't want to use alcohol or drugs. Just because you were born into a situation doesn't mean that situation has to be born into you.

Educate yourself about alcohol and drugs, and maybe you can educate the ones you love in turn. I believe in you, and I know you are a winner, in life and over drugs.

7

Life
Lessons

ROLE MODELS

I T IS IMPORTANT WHEN YOU ARE GROWING UP TO have someone you can look up to and admire, someone you can trust and believe in. There were many people outside of my family that I thought of as role models. Three in particular come to mind: Mr. and Mrs. Golden and Ms. Augustine.

The Goldens were our neighbors; they lived around the block from us. Every school day, my bus would stop in front of my house, but I would leave thirty minutes early just so I could walk around the corner and pick up my friends Lisa and Victor Golden. I liked walking to the bus stop with Lisa and Vic because we would talk about school and things and it was a relaxing way to start the day. More than walking with them, I enjoyed the special attention their parents would pay to me. Every morning they would ask me how I was and what I was up too. They really seemed interested, and they always had positive or constructive advice to give me. Mr. Golden would say, "When I was your age, I would do so-and-so." Then Mrs. Golden would say, "Charles, leave that girl alone. She doesn't want to hear about you a hundred years ago." I would laugh and tell her I didn't mind.

Mrs. Golden would always have a vitamin with a glass of orange juice waiting for me on the breakfast table. They treated me like I was one of their own children. Even after I had grown up, whenever I saw them they were (and still are) curious about what I was doing, and occasionally Mr. Golden would tell me a story about when he was a child. Sometimes Mrs. Golden still checks to see if I'm taking my vitamins.

My other outside-the-family role model was Ms. Augustine, my ninth grade Sunday school teacher. All my life I went to Sunday school, and as a child I always found it interesting. But when I hit adolescence, I started to get bored with the classes and would barely pay attention. Then we switched churches and I met Ms. Augustine.

She was a small lady with a very intelligent sounding voice. At first I thought, "Oh, no, not another boring teacher who is going to lecture us!" But Ms. Augustine was different from the very first day. She started class with the question, "What is God like to a teenager?" I thought, "Hey! This isn't the typical Sunday-school question. Someone consult the rule book!"

Ms. Augustine made every class interesting for us by tying it in with our everyday lives. "After all," she said, "God is an everyday, every-person God. He knows what it's like to be a teenager." I had never thought of that before. I had always pictured God as an old person who only knew old sayings and events. But Ms. Augustine showed us how He knew us and, even better, that He knew *me,* Cassandra Walker. Before long, I couldn't wait to get to Ms. Augustine's class. I wanted to tell her how I had taken what I learned in the previous class and applied it to my week.

She often told us to "practice what you preach." If we told others to be courteous, then we were supposed to be courteous, too. This was very difficult for me sometimes. I could say the right things, but once I got to school and was tempted by gossip and cheating, I had to really work hard to practice what I preached.

I remember when one boy in our class was upset because someone had been mean to him and he wanted to be mean back. Ms. Augustine told him, "Stick to your values and never change to the negative. Especially when you know it's wrong or you're doing something just to get back at someone." We all learned that day that being a good person was something we had to work at, but when we did, we could be sure that good things eventually would happen back to us.

One Sunday morning I went rushing into class to see Ms. Augustine and found a man there instead. He announced that he was our new teacher. Our whole class was devastated. Later, in church, I saw Ms. Augustine and asked her why she was leaving. She explained that she had been asked to make some changes in her teaching style, and rather than do that, she had decided to resign. She told me that our new teacher was nice and I would like him.

I continued to go to Sunday school but it wasn't the same. Soon almost all of the teens stopped coming except for me and another girl. I never found out exactly what happened to make Ms. Augustine quit teaching, but I know that she loved us too much to sacrifice her style. She had often told us that she would not compromise when something she believed in was at stake. For that reason, and for her other wonderful attributes, she will always be one of my role models.

GOSSIP, GOSSIP, GOSSIP

Hey, did you hear about....
Girl, I heard that....
Did you know that....

THESE ARE JUST SOME OF THE WAYS IT STARTS— with a statement or question followed by a bunch of words that are half-true, if at all. The goal is to purposely hurt or tear down other individuals.

Gossip, gossip, gossip.

I must admit that I used to like to listen to gossip. Most times, I didn't believe what I was hearing because the source of the material was so vague. "I know this is true," a friend of mine would say, "because my cousin's sister's boyfriend's aunt told her, and you know that she knows everything." Yeah, right.

I soon learned that where there was gossip you could always find its friends, jealousy, envy, anger, and lies. Most gossip, if not all, starts and continues because of someone's jealousy, envy, or anger. Think about some of the most recent gossip you have heard, and I'll bet you will find that behind that story are lies, anger, and jealousy mixed in with envy.

Gossip is a small word with big consequences and it spreads faster than a sleek jetliner flies. The difference is that gossip *always* arrives at its destination way off schedule and all mixed up.

I remember a time when I was in the eighth grade and some gossip I started caught up with me. I had decided to try out for cheerleading. The coach was a P.E. teacher who taught my afternoon gym class. I had tried out for cheerleading the year before and was cut. This year was no exception. Luckily for me, there were pom-pon try-outs just one week after I learned that I hadn't made the cheerleading squad.

I decided to go out for pom-pons. When the final list of everyone who had made the squad was posted on the girls' locker room door, I saw that I had made it. My name was at the end of the list, but at least it was on the list. Then the cheerleading coach said, "Well, Cassandra, you made it. Your name is the last one on the list. It looks like you were almost cut from this squad, too."

"How rude!" I thought. I didn't say anything to her at the time, but she had hurt my feelings. Later that day, I overheard some other girls talking about the cheerleading coach. They said she thought the pom-pon squad was just a bunch of cheerleading rejects.

Even though I hadn't heard the coach say that, it sounded like something she *might* say, so I started telling people that she really *had* said it. By the next day, the story was all over the school, and everyone on the pom-pon squad—including the coach—was upset. In fact, the pom-pon coach was so upset that she told the cheerleading coach how she felt and why. Uh-oh!

Some of my more loose-lipped "friends" thought it their civic duty to tell that I had started the rumor. At gym class that day, I was called into the cheerleading coach's office. She scolded me and asked why I would spread such a rumor and get so many people angry at her. "I didn't mean to get you into trouble," I answered, "but I was mad at you because you said that mean thing to me about being the last person on the pom-pons list. I wanted to get back at you." She reprimanded me, made me confess to my pom-pon coach, and that was the end of it as far as discipline was concerned.

Even though that incident was eventually over and done with, I still remember how I hurt someone. When I took my anger and turned it around by lying, it didn't help at all. Wait, I take that back: It taught me the effects of gossip. It also taught me that when you gossip and the fire gets too hot, don't look to your friends for support.

This is a saying I made up to help me try to avoid gossip. You can use it, too:

Garbage
Outpoured to
Simply
Scar
Innocent
People.

NOT MY FAVORITE TEACHER!

THERE ARE CERTAIN PEOPLE WHO, FOR ONE reason or another, have a fond place in our memories. For me, one of these people was my junior year English teacher. In the beginning, none of us knew much about him. I believe it was his first year teaching at my high school.

On the first day of class, he had us introduce ourselves and tell something interesting about ourselves. I don't remember what I said, but when his time came around he told us that he loved vocabulary words. "By the end of the school year," he promised, "you will, too."

He gave us a vocabulary test every week. I didn't like the fact that we had to take the tests, but soon I noticed the difference in my conversations. I started to recognize words that I had normally blocked out because I didn't know their meanings. I could hold conversations with adults and not feel intimidated.

Some of the vocabulary words were strange and dealt a lot with the human body. I didn't quite understand why we needed to know them, but I was enjoying increasing my language abilities.

The teacher gave us fun assignments, like picking teams and having a spell-offs on some of the words we learned. He assigned us interesting reports to write and read them out loud to the class for constructive criticism. This may sound cruel, but it motivated me to do my research and write my very best.

We saw the movie *Hair* and had a lengthy conversation about what it meant in the 1960's and what it meant in our society. By then, we all felt that our teacher was a great teacher and a great individual. He was the first teacher to allow boys to be on the pom-pon squad. He even turned it into a male-female drill team that won numerous awards and trophies.

When the school year ended, I was very sad to leave his class. I hugged him and wished him well. After that, whenever I saw him I smiled, gave him a big hug, and asked him how his life was. Even after I graduated, I visited my high school just to see him and talk to him.

One day, while I was in college, my aunt called me and told me that my favorite teacher was in the news. I became excited and asked her why. Had he won an award? Been promoted to principal? Was he nominated for Teacher of the Year and on his way to meet the President of the United States?

My aunt interrupted me. "He has been arrested for molesting male students at your old high school." I was devastated.

My first reaction was "Not my favorite teacher! They must have the wrong man! It's a setup!" But as the weeks went by and the newspapers started printing the story, I learned that the story was true. My favorite teacher had a serious problem. He was having sex with some of the boys in exchange for better grades. I felt sick inside—for him, and especially for the boys who were his victims. My favorite teacher had taken advantage of them. They would suffer for the rest of their lives.

He went to court and eventually, I think, to prison. Since it was found during the trial that the boys had "consented" to have sex with their teacher, he only did a little time. Last I heard, he was working for some company and no longer teaching.

Things would be different today. As a society, we're more savvy than we were ten years ago about sexual abuse. We are a lot less likely to "blame the victim." Abusers are getting longer prison sentences. We recognize now that abusers are sick and need help, but first and foremost they must prevented from abusing anyone else. We also recognize that victims need to know that it's okay to tell someone when they are being abused. They need to know that the abuse is never, ever their fault.

I thought about my teacher a lot both during and after the trial. Gradually some things became clear to me. Some of those strange vocabulary words that dealt with the human body. Some of the inappropriate language in the movie *Hair*. They had all been signs that something wasn't right. If we had known what those signs meant, if we had spoken up to another teacher or the principal or the school counselor or our parents, those boys might not have been abused.

I hope my teacher got the help he needed. I hope the boys got the help *they* needed.

If you are ever in a situation where you feel that something isn't right—if you ever hear that a friend is being abused—I hope you will have the courage to say something about it. If you are ever abused yourself, be sure to tell an adult you trust. If that person doesn't help you, tell someone else. You have a right for the abuse to stop.

ODOR PROBLEM

THE GIRLS' LOCKER ROOM IN JUNIOR HIGH school was very crowded. I remember having to wait for some girls to get into their gym suits before I could even start getting into mine. There was just not enough room for everyone. Sometimes I would develop a headache as all of the cheap perfume we wore blended together and formed a slight smog.

There was something else that caused discomfort for me and a lot of the other girls: the very strong odor that came from one of our classmates. It never failed. Katie (not her real name) would start undressing, and everyone else would start coughing and covering their noses. Some people were just being cruel, but it really was such a terrible odor that you wanted to cover your nose. Katie knew we were talking about her, but she kept undressing as if nothing was wrong.

Some girls started poking fun at her and asking things like "Is your shower broken at home?" or "Did your family run out of soap?" She didn't respond.

I felt ashamed when I laughed at some of the mean jokes and statements that were made about her. Then one day another girl asked us to take up an offering to buy Katie some soap and deodorant. "This is not a joke," she insisted. "I really think she needs them." I agreed and believed she was serious, so we all pitched in some money.

The next day we all watched as the girl approached Katie, gave a small speech, and presented her with our gift. We stood around gawking. At the time, I thought it was the right thing to do.

Katie started crying and shaking. She was so upset that the gym teacher came out of her office and asked us what was going on. We told her and she gave us an angry look. Then she took Katie into her office.

We found out later that Katie had a problem inside her body that caused the terrible odor. It wasn't because she didn't keep herself clean. She must have been so offended and hurt by our actions. I felt terrible.

Much to our dismay, Katie had a great attitude for the rest of the school year. She never held a grudge, and she still spoke to us. Once we knew the truth, her odor didn't seem as strong anymore. There were still a few mean girls who would say something cruel from time to time, but Katie just ignored them.

I learned three things from this experience. First, if someone you know has an odor problem, don't take it upon yourself to tell the person unless you are very good friends. Second, tell the person in private, or ask a teacher or the school nurse to talk to him or her. Finally, I realized that something was stinking even more than my classmate: my attitude.

Treat people the way you want to be treated and you will never go wrong.

REMEMBERING BRAD

THE SUMMER BEFORE I STARTED THE FIFTH grade, my brother and I became friends with a new boy in the neighborhood named Brad. My brother liked him because he was tough and could play sports with him. I liked him because I thought he was cute. In fact, just about every girl in the neighborhood thought he was cute. He had dark curly hair and big brown eyes. He was a total dreamboat. Unfortunately, he had absolutely no interest in girls, especially me.

I remember how he used to tease me and call me "Skinny Minnie." For some reason, I didn't get as mad at him for teasing me as I did at the other boys.

Brad had a cousin who was 18 years old. Every time his cousin came to see him, Brad would brag to us about him. Brad's cousin must have served as a father figure for him, and that is why he always got so excited when he visited. You see, Brad didn't have a father. I think his father died, but I'm not sure. He lived with his mother and little brother, Clowny. If his brother had another name, no one knew it. We all just called him Clowny.

Anyway, Brad kept talking all summer about how he and his cousin were going to the Indianapolis 500 speedway in August. I must admit that my brother and I were jealous. We knew how much fun he was going to have. Our family had a vacation planned also; we were going to Florida for three weeks in late July. Before we left, Brad told us that by the time we got back he would have already gone to the Indianapolis 500 and he would tell us about it. We said good-bye and went on our way.

When we returned home, we couldn't wait to hear about Brad's trip. As we started to walk to his house, a friend of ours stopped us and said, "Brad is missing." "What do you mean, missing?" we wanted to know. Our friend went on to tell us how Brad and his cousin had gone to Indiana but never returned. It had been two weeks since anyone had heard from them.

We couldn't believe it. We were shocked. In the back of my mind, I kept telling myself that he would come knocking on our door any day now with the long, drawn-out story of his trip. But days turned into weeks and soon the school year started and there was still no sign of Brad or his cousin. I kept expecting to see him hanging out of his bedroom window yelling at me, "Hey, Skinny Minnie, whatcha doin'?"

Several months passed by. Meanwhile Brad's brother Clowny would walk up and down the street with a sad and lonely look on his face. Then one cold day in November I saw police cars parked outside of Brad's house.

"They found him!" I shouted. I couldn't wait to see him. My mother went over his house shortly after the police left. My brother and I could hardly wait for her to come home and tell us that we could go see our friend. After about half an hour, my mother returned. Her eyes were red and her makeup smeared. She sat us down and said, "They found Brad." Our eyes opened wide and our hearts started pounding like drums. "He is dead," she said.

All of a sudden I screamed, "No! Kids don't die!" Then I started crying uncontrollably. My mother went on to tell us what the police had told Brad's mother.

Brad and his cousin had been traveling home from Indiana when their car was sideswiped and went off the bridge road and into the Calumet River. They were trapped inside the car and couldn't get out. Their bodies were so badly decomposed that Brad's mother had to identify him by the clothes he was wearing and his dental records.

We were devastated. I felt like someone had taken my heart and squeezed it. It hurt deep down into my soul. When I looked at my brother, he wasn't crying. He was just staring at the floor, not saying a word.

I couldn't understand why a beautiful young boy like Brad had to die so tragically, his life snuffed out for no reason. I had thought that kids lived forever, or at least until they were adults.

The next day my mother, brother, and I took some food over to Brad's mother's house. Brad's mother, who usually was so bubbly and upbeat, sat quietly with her head down. Clowny's face was blank and he looked like he had no life in him. I could only wonder what was going through his mind. First he had no father, and now his big brother was gone. I could barely look at him.

They had the funeral the next day. I couldn't bring myself to go. My mother and my brother went. When they came home, my brother told me that Brad's casket had been closed and his school picture had been on top of the casket. Then my brother asked me to follow him to his room.

He shut the door behind us, looked me in the eyes, and started crying. It dawned on me that this was the first time my brother had cried since we learned about Brad's death. "I just kept telling myself that Brad wasn't dead, he was just living somewhere else," my brother said through his tears. "But when I went to the funeral, I knew it was true."

My brother and I said a prayer for Brad and his family. We held each others' hands and cried together. Then we made the decision to tear up Brad's obituary and put the pain behind us. We looked at Brad's smiling face one more time and kissed him. Then we ripped up the obituary into little pieces and threw them away.

It has been many years since Brad died, but every so often I think about him and his mother and brother. Just recently my mother told me that whenever she goes over the Calumet bridge, she thinks about Brad, too. I have gone through several more deaths of friends and relatives since then, but none has affected me like the first death of a friend.

Soon after the funeral, my mother sat us down and told us that dying was just as much a part of life as living was. She told us that we had to go on living and enjoying each other and our friends, always remembering to let the people we loved know that we loved them. This way, when they died, we would know in our hearts that we had treated them kindly and with love.

Although I was able to live with Brad's death and go on with my life, it still gives me pleasure to know that somewhere in Heaven there is a curly-haired, brown-eyed boy saying, "Hey, Skinny Minnie, whatcha doin'?"

SEX EDUCATION

IN ABOUT THE SIXTH OR SEVENTH GRADE, SCHOOLS start showing health films about the makeup of the male and female bodies. At least, this is when my school started. Unfortunately, since sex is such a sensitive subject, my school just kind of skipped around the answer to the question of how a female becomes pregnant.

In the eighth grade, we were all excited to be almost 13. This meant we could legally be called "teenagers," which to us equaled "almost grown up." It meant being able to go to bed a little later, pick out all of your own school clothes, and watch PG-rated movies. For one girl in our class, it meant being pregnant.

Back then I didn't know how a person gets pregnant, and I had never seen a pregnant person up close. So when the rumor started about this girl, I assumed it was just a rumor with no substance. Besides, we were still kids, and kids couldn't have babies.

Then one day I noticed that this girl, who was on the pom-pon team with me, was starting to look a little plump around the middle. When the coach asked her "Are you pregnant?"—in front of the whole squad—she said "No, I have the stomach mumps." To me, that seemed like a reasonable explanation as to why she had suddenly gained so much weight. I had never heard of the stomach mumps, but it made perfect sense to me.

A few weeks later, she was cut from the squad, and the rumor was confirmed: She was indeed pregnant. "How could this be?" I thought. "Only mommies who are much older get pregnant." And "What about the husband? Where is he? Surely she is too young to be married."

The school did a poor job of handling this situation. After a few months, when it was very obvious that the girl was pregnant, the teachers wouldn't even talk about it, at least not to us. They just tried to act as if her pregnancy didn't exist, or worse, they would shake their heads when the girl walked by. They treated her like a criminal. Even then I knew that being pregnant at an early age was serious, but it certainly wasn't a crime.

The other students didn't know what to make of it. We just started guessing how this could have happened. "I heard that if you eat watermelon seeds, you could become pregnant," someone said. "I heard that if you drink water right after a boy, this can make you pregnant," someone else added. The situation left us all baffled and wanting the right answers.

The girl went on to have the baby and raise her. I don't know what she is up to now, but I know that she jumped into being a mother and missed the chance to be a child. As I went through junior high and high school, there were several more teenage pregnancies. Some girls got pregnant out of ignorance. Others got pregnant out of loneliness and the desire to have someone to love and be loved by.

There were probably other reasons I didn't know about, but whatever the reasons were, those girls all got pregnant too young, and their lives were changed forever.

Mistakes happen in life. If you find yourself in this situation, remember that there are people who love you and organizations that can help you. If at all possible, talk to your parents or another adult you trust. If you don't feel you have anyone you can talk to, there are shelters and counselors in every state. You might want to start by checking with your school counselor. What's important is to get help right now. You also need to get educated so you don't repeat the same mistake.

If you know a young girl who is pregnant, don't just stare at her and talk about her behind her back. Try to be her friend. Believe me, that is what she needs right now. You teachers out there, please take the chance to ask the child if she needs to talk. If it is possible to do this in your school—if there aren't rules against it—bring up the subject in class and help the other students understand it.

Whoever you are—a student, teacher, neighbor, or friend—keep an open mind and try not to judge. Judging won't help a pregnant teen to put her life back together again.

OUT TOO FAR

I STARTED TAKING SWIMMING LESSONS WHEN I WAS three years old. My mother once told me that when I was in preschool I jumped into the deep end (13 feet) at a local swimming pool. She said she almost had a heart attack. I guess I have always been sort of a daredevil.

During the summer when I was 12, my family and I went to Virginia Beach, Virginia, to visit my grandmother. She lived just two miles from the Atlantic ocean beach front. When we arrived, my father called me, my brother, and our cousin together for a serious talk about swimming in the ocean.

"When I was a little boy, I almost drowned there," he told us. "The waves are dangerous. They can sneak up on you if you are not careful." I thought to myself, "You were a less experienced swimmer than me, so no wonder you had trouble."

We kids were anxious to go to the beach, so we didn't really listen to my father. Soon he took us to a local store and bought us an inflatable raft. He told us to stay in the shallow end of the water and float on the raft. That way we wouldn't have to worry about the waves and he wouldn't have to worry about us. I just nodded my head, still not listening.

When we got to the beach, we all ran into the water and started playing. My brother didn't really like swimming all that much, so he stayed on the raft most of the time. I decided that I wanted to look around, so I went out to where the water came to just below my armpits. I could see the waves rolling in and I would ride them in a little and relax as they pushed me out some into the ocean. Each time I would end up about the same spot in the water.

I could see my brother and cousin floating on the raft, and we waved at each other. Then I noticed a gigantic wave approaching. It rose up about ten feet above my head. I held my breath and waited to coast on its impact and power. The wave hit and pushed me. It was like riding a roller coaster. Then I felt the current switch and my body was being pulled out into the cool ocean. When I finally stopped moving, I stood up to see if my brother had seen me take that last wave.

When my feet hit the soft, sandy bottom of the ocean, I could feel sea shells in between my toes. I tried to look over the water, but my head went under and all I could see was the murky water. I tried again, and this time I had to jump to see over the water. Then I realized that I was out too deep. Before I knew it, another wave came and pulled me out even further. I started to panic as I gasped for air. I could see my brother and cousin far off in the distance, playing on the raft. I tried to call them, but I was too weak and water entered my mouth.

I went down for the third time and I felt the water suffocating me. I couldn't lift my body up, and I started to sink under the pressure of the waves. I could hear my father's voice telling me to beware of the waves as another wave forced me even further out. I closed my eyes and said a prayer.

Suddenly something huge pulled me up and over the water. I started coughing and gagging. I saw a man with a bright smile. He asked me to hold on to him and relax. He took me back to the shore, where my brother had finally noticed me and come over to see what was happening. By the time we got to the shore, I had caught my breath and gotten a little of my energy back.

The man set me down on the beach and made sure I was okay. Then he left. I have never seen him since. I don't know who he was—he wasn't a lifeguard—but I do know that he saved my life.

I learned a lesson that day that I still remember as an adult: The life experiences of others can be helpful to us. When my father tried to warn me about the ocean's waves, and when he told me about what had happened to him as a boy, I should have listened. His life experience could have saved me from almost dying.

Has a parent, guardian, or friend ever tried to tell you something he or she knew was important, but you didn't really listen? Has something

happened to you like what happened to me? If so, I hope you learned (like I did) that life is too important to ignore the rules just because we think we know all there is to know.

Do me a favor. The next time someone gives you instructions or advice, even if you would rather not hear it, take the time to listen. Then really think about what you were told. See if it just might make sense.

ABOUT THE AUTHOR

ASSANDRA WALKER SIMMONS IS A YOUTH reporter and host of "Youth Corner" for WCCO TV in Minneapolis, Minnesota. She is a popular speaker on self-esteem at schools and businesses, and she hosts a talk show for teens and young adults called "Express Yourself" on the nationally syndicated Radio AAHS. Her company, By Faith, manufactures and markets Self-Esteem Wear T-shirts with positive messages.

Cassandra received her B.A. in Mass Communications from Western Illinois University. She worked as a newspaper reporter, public relations director, English teacher, and public speaker before moving to television and radio. She and her husband, Scott, and their sons, Scott II and Skyler Julius, live in Minneapolis.

NOTES

NOTES

NOTES

404 762 4066

762 4847

Nancy Robinson

Book

Stories From My Life

Cassandra Walker

$6.95

Kids with Courage
True Stories about Young People Making a Difference
by Barbara A. Lewis

Exciting true accounts of kids taking social action, fighting crime, working to save the environment, and performing heroic acts. Ages 11 and up.
160 pp; B&W photos; s/c; 6" x 9"
ISBN 0-915793-39-3; $10.95

Making the Most of Today
Daily Readings for Young People on Self-Awareness, Creativity, and Self-Esteem

by Pamela Espeland and Rosemary Wallner

Quotes from sources such as Mariah Carey, Martin Luther King, Jr., and "Calvin and Hobbes" help guide young people through a year of positive thinking, problem-solving, and practical lifeskills. Ages 11 and up.
392 pp; s/c; 4" x 7"
ISBN 0-915793-33-4; $8.95

School Power
Strategies for Succeeding in School
by Jeanne Shay Schumm, Ph.D.
and Marguerite Radencich, Ph.D.

Covers getting organized, taking notes, studying smarter, writing better, following directions, handling homework, managing long-term assignments, and much more. Ages 11 and up.
132 pp; illus.; B&W photos; s/c; 8 1/2" x 11"
ISBN 0-915793-42-3; $11.95

To place an order, or to request a free catalog of SELF-HELP FOR KIDS® materials, write or call:

Free Spirit Publishing Inc.
400 First Avenue North, Suite 616
Minneapolis, MN 55401-1730
toll-free (800)735-7323, local (612)338-2068